D1744221

BOOK ANALYSIS

Written by Nadège Nicolas and Johanna Biehler

Translated by Soline de Dorlodot and Emma Hanna

The Alchemist
BY PAULO COELHO

Bright
≡Summaries.com

PAULO COELHO

BRAZILIAN WRITER AND LYRICIST

- **Born in Rio de Janeiro in 1947.**
- **Notable works:**
  - *The Pilgrimage* (1987), novel
  - *Veronika Decides to Die* (1998), novel
  - *The Devil and Miss Prym* (2000), novel

Paulo Coelho was born in Rio de Janeiro in 1947. At the age of 23, he left Brazil to travel through South America (Mexico, Peru, Bolivia, Chile), Europe and North Africa. He returned to Brazil two years later and began working in the music industry, first as a writer of pop songs, then as a journalist specialising in Brazilian music and eventually as an employee at the American music label PolyGram. However, the lure of travelling and his desire for spiritual fulfilment proved irresistible, and he set off again in 1982.

His first successful novel, *The Pilgrimage* (1987), was inspired by his own experience on the Camino de Santiago (a popular Christian pilgrimage route in Spain). Coelho has continued to publish regularly in the intervening years, and his work has been well received by the general public and the literary world alike: he won *Elle* magazine's Reader's Choice Award in 1995 and was elected to the Brazilian Academy of Letters in 2002.

THE ALCHEMIST

A SPIRITUAL QUEST

- **Genre:** philosophical novel
- **Reference edition:** Coelho, P. (2012) *The Alchemist*. Trans. Clarke, A. R. London: HarperCollins.
- **1st edition:** 1988
- **Themes:** mysticism, journey, religion, identity, quest, coming-of-age

The Alchemist tells the story of Santiago, a young Andalusian shepherd who leaves his sheep and his homeland in search of the treasure he believes is buried at the foot of the Pyramids in Egypt. The young man has many encounters and experiences along the way, all of which lead him towards the treasure he seeks while also helping him to discover himself.

The Alchemist is a philosophical novel which was inspired by a short story by Jorge Luis Borges (Argentinian writer, 1899-1986), and champions the message that everyone is free to follow their own dreams and make them a reality. It has been published in 150 countries and translated into over 50 languages, making it one of the bestselling novels of all time.

SUMMARY

The first scene of the novel depicts the alchemist discovering a book of short stories by Oscar Wilde (Irish writer, 1854-1900). He reads one story inspired by the legend of Narcissus, but with a different ending: in Greek mythology, Narcissus was a handsome young man who fell in love with his own reflection, and was so distraught by his inability to capture it that he wasted away and died. However, in this tale the lake mourns the young man's death, but only because it loved to gaze at its own reflection in the young man's eyes.

One night, an inquisitive young shepherd called Santiago decides to stop at an old church and spend the night there. He is looking forward to being reunited with the young woman he had fallen in love with the year before. The tale of how they met is told via a flashback, which is followed by a second flashback which explains Santiago's decision to take control of his own fate by becoming a shepherd so that he can discover the world.

That night, he dreams that a child is leading him to the Pyramids of Egypt and that she tells him: "If you come here, you will find a hidden treasure" (p. 13). Even though Santiago wakes up before she can show him the treasure's exact location, this dream convinces him to embark on the long journey from Andalusia to Giza.

In Tarifa (Spain), a fortune-teller agrees to interpret this dream, but she asks for a tenth of the treasure in exchange, and tells him that it is a very difficult dream to interpret because it is in the language of the world. Santiago is disappointed by her interpretation, and sets off again.

After this encounter, he is approached by an old man called Melchizedek who claims to be the king of Salem and who offers to tell him how to find the hidden treasure in exchange for a tenth of his herd. According to him, the treasure is the shepherd's destiny, and he explains that a person's destiny is their life's purpose. The old man's words convince Santiago to set off on his quest. They meet again the next day, and the king advises Santiago to pay attention to the signs and to make all his own decisions from now on. To help him do so, the king gives him two divination stones called Urim and Thummim.

Santiago then sells his herd and goes to Tangier in Morocco. He does not understand Arabic, which is the language spoken there, or the local customs, which he describes as "practice[s] of infidels" (p. 32). His naïveté leads to his money being stolen, and he is so overwhelmed that he is on the verge of giving up until the divination stones give him a surge of fresh hope, after which he decides to follow the signs and continue his journey.

The next day, he meets a crystal merchant and cleans his goods in exchange for food. The merchant eventually suggests that Santiago keep working for him until he earns enough money to continue his quest. Santiago is determined to do whatever it takes to fulfil his destiny, so he agrees to stay for as long as he needs to.

During this time, he tries to suggest ways that his employer could improve his business, but the merchant is resistant to change as he does not see the need for it. He questions the young shepherd about his motivation for travelling to the Pyramids when he could just build one in his garden, to which Santiago replies: "You've never had dreams of travel" (p. 51).

The merchant then explains the five pillars of Islam, one of which is a pilgrimage to Mecca (Saudi Arabia). He says that he prefers dreaming about this journey instead of going on it, because he is afraid that once he makes this dream a reality, he will no longer have anything to live for.

Almost a year after he first arrived, Santiago tells the merchant that he is leaving. He sets off again, and along the way he meets an Englishman who is looking for an alchemist. They both travel towards Al-Fayoum (Egypt) in the same caravan, and the Englishman lends Santiago his books about alchemy, but the only thing the shepherd understands is that all of the books share one common idea: "all things are the manifestation of one thing only." (p. 76)

Santiago also has a conversation with a camel driver, who tells him that a clan war is brewing, but that he fears nothing because he lives solely in the present ("Because I don't live in either my past or my future. I'm interested only in the present", p. 81). This idea greatly influences

Santiago's future behaviour.

The caravan arrives at the oasis where the alchemist is staying. While looking for him, Santiago meets a girl called Fatima and falls in love with her. After spending some time with her, he is tempted to abandon his quest. Later, while watching hawks soaring through the sky, the shepherd has a vision of an imminent battle. He recounts it to the tribe leader, and when it comes true he is made a counsellor.

When the dust has settled, Santiago goes to visit the alchemist, who reminds him that he must fulfil his destiny to give meaning to everything he has lived through up to this point. Seeing that the shepherd has doubts, the alchemist tells him what his life will be like if he decides to give up. That night, Santiago tells Fatima that he is leaving. She does not try to stop him, and decides to wait for him.

The alchemist travels through the desert with Santiago and teaches him to listen to his heart. He also teaches him the language of the world and encourages him to follow every sign he sees. Along the way, they run into a group of soldiers who accuse them of being spies, and Santiago's companion introduces the shepherd as an alchemist who can turn himself into wind. The soldiers want to see this miracle, but the travelling companions explain that they need three days to prepare.

Three days later, the shepherd successfully performs this feat by calling upon the desert, the wind, the sun and, finally, "the hand that wrote all" (p. 144). The wind begins blowing so fiercely that "[f]or generations thereafter, the Arabs recounted the legend of a boy who had turned himself into the wind, almost destroying a military camp, in defiance of the most powerful chief in the desert" (pp. 145-146).

They arrive at a monastery where the alchemist demonstrates how to turn lead into gold. He divides the metal into four parts: one for himself, one for Santiago, and two for the monk they meet there (one to thank him, and the other in case the young shepherd needs it in the future).

Santiago arrives at the Pyramids, where he lets himself be guided by his heart. It whispers to him: "Be aware of the place where you are brought to tears. That's where I am, and that's where your treasure is" (p. 152).

He begins digging at the spot his heart has led him to, where he is attacked. He eventually admits to his attackers that he is looking for treasure that he saw in a dream. One of the men replies that he is stupid and inadvertently tells the young man where the treasure actually is: buried under the sycamore tree beside the old church in Andalusia where the young shepherd had slept before he set out on his pilgrimage. Santiago decides to go there.

Along the way, he thinks back on the path he followed to reach his treasure, and remembers that he has to give a tenth of it to the fortune-teller. The wind starts blowing, and brings him a kiss from Fatima.

CHARACTER STUDY

SANTIAGO

The novel's protagonist is Santiago, a young Andalusian man who decided to become a shepherd two years before the story begins because he wanted to see the world. This brought him into conflict with his parents, who wanted him to become a monk. He has an inquisitive streak and a thirst for knowledge, and is constantly looking for new paths to follow when he is travelling with his sheep.

He believes that nothing is more important that fulfilling one's destiny, meaning the unique dream that all of us harbour deep inside, which can only be achieved if we are willing and able to fight for our deepest desires: "It's the possibility of having a dream come true that makes life interesting" (p. 10).

Like everyone else, Santiago's life has its highs and lows, and he is no stranger to self-doubt. However, he pays great attention to the signs and displays the courage and strength of will to make his dreams a reality. Although he sometimes loses heart, this never lasts long and he always finds a new reason to keep moving forward. For example, when the crystal merchant tells him that the journey to Egypt is too expensive for him, Santiago quickly changes his goal and agrees to work until he makes enough money to buy more sheep.

Santiago listens to the world around him and to his own heart, and symbolises every individual's capacity to dream. One of his most distinctive personality traits is his childlike openness towards others and towards life itself. As they grow up, adults tend to forget their true desires or bury them deep inside themselves by dismissing them as childish and incompatible with a "reasonable" attitude. However, Santiago reminds us that our fate is in our own hands and that following our dreams is always worthwhile.

THE ALCHEMIST

Even though the novel is named after the alchemist, his character always remains shrouded in mystery: his name, age and origins are never revealed to the reader (although the Englishman says that he is "two hundred years old", p. 113). His physical appearance is never described in detail either, aside from one brief description when Santiago first meets him:

> "Astride the animal was a horseman dressed completely in black, with a falcon perched on his left shoulder. He wore a turban and his entire face, except for his eyes, was covered with a black kerchief. He appeared to be a messenger from the desert, but his presence was much more powerful than that of a mere messenger." (p. 104)

His only defining characteristics are his profession as an alchemist and his ability to interpret signs. His sole function within the story is to guide Santiago in his quest to fulfil his destiny, even though this is totally unrelated to the traditional definition of alchemy. The young shepherd sees him as a mentor, and he simply points him "in the direction of [his] treasure" (p. 110).

However, he acts differently towards the Englishman who wants to become an alchemist himself, as the alchemist believes that he is not yet ready. Instead of helping him directly, he encourages him to start taking more action without revealing any of his "trade secrets" in the process. He is a true alchemist, not a charlatan, having learned the science from his forebears, and uses "a small crystal flask filled with a liquid, and a yellow glass egg that was slightly larger than a chicken's egg" (p. 127) to move around, which he describes as "the Master Work of the alchemists" (p. 128).

ALCHEMY

Alchemy is a field of research which was popular during the Middle Ages and the Renaissance. It focuses on the transmutation of metals and the search for the panacea (a miraculous cure-all). Its practitioners sought to create the Philosopher's Stone (sometimes known as the Magnum Opus, or Master Work), a mythical object believed to be capable of turning common metals like lead into gold and producing the Elixir of Life. Although Nicolas Flamel (French scribe and bookseller, c. 1330-1418) is the best-known of their number, he was never a true alchemist; his immense fortune simply led his peers to believe that it had been created using the Philosopher's Stone.

Although chemistry was simply considered a byword for alchemy for centuries, they eventually evolved into two distinct fields of study: chemistry came to be seen as a real science, whereas alchemy is considered an esoteric or even magical pseudoscience.

THE OLD FORTUNE-TELLER

The fortune-teller is the first person Santiago meets in Tarifa. He asks her to shed some light on the meaning of his dream about the treasure, and she agrees to forego being paid directly in exchange for a tenth of the treasure. She claims that it is very difficult to interpret this kind of dream, but in the end she tells the young shepherd nothing new. To justify herself, she explains to Santiago that "[i]t's the simple things in life that are the most extraordinary" (p. 14).

MELCHIZEDEK, KING OF SALEM

Although Melchizedek disguises himself as a destitute old man, he wears a golden breastplate studded with gemstones hidden underneath his rags. He approaches Santiago and offers to tell him how to reach the treasure in exchange for a tenth of his herd. He then proves that he is not a charlatan by writing the names of the shepherd's parents and an account of his whole life in the sand, even "things that [Santiago] had never told anyone" (p. 20).

This character plays a key role in Santiago's quest, because he is the one who convinces him to set off on it. He is also the one who introduces the concept of destiny and the "principle of favorability" (p. 27), or beginner's luck, and he gives Santiago two divination stones called Urim and Thummim.

THE CRYSTAL MERCHANT

Santiago works for the crystal merchant in Tangier for nearly a year. The merchant has never made the pilgrimage to Mecca, and does not intend to, because dreaming about this journey has become his reason for living, which he would lose if he ever made the dream a reality. He is accustomed to his quiet little life, and does not appreciate Santiago's innovative ideas to improve his business, but when he eventually gives in, his profits soar.

THE ENGLISHMAN

Santiago meets the Englishman when they travel together in the same caravan. He is looking for the alchemist, who will be able to help him decipher a code and discover how to make the Elixir of Life and the Philosopher's Stone. His books are his sole reason for living and he pays no attention to the world until he meets the alchemist at the oasis. From then on, he begins paying attention to the desert, and is no longer content to simply read his books. This is when he realises that he must start taking action without fear of failure. In this way, he takes another step towards fulfilling his destiny.

FATIMA

Santiago falls in love with this young woman from the desert. She is conscious of her role and knows that her destiny is to wait for the shepherd at the oasis. Santiago is tempted to stay by her side, but the alchemist makes it clear to him that if he abandons his quest, he and Fatima will be miserable. On the contrary, if their love is pure they will find each other again, no matter what.

ANALYSIS

A COMING-OF-AGE NOVEL

A young hero searching for himself

A coming-of-age novel follows a single character's evolution as their understanding of the world develops, which often leads them to discover their true self after overcoming a series of obstacles. This genre, which is also known as the *Bildungsroman*, emerged in Germany in the 18th century, and generally addresses "the processes by which a sensitive soul discovers its identity and its role in the big world" (*Britannica*). It can therefore be defined as "[a] story of the emergence of a personality and a talent, with its implicit motifs of struggle, conflict, suffering, and success" (*ibid.*).

Wilhelm Meister's Apprenticeship (1795-1796) by Johann Wolfgang von Goethe (German writer, 1749-1832) is generally considered the flagship work of this genre.

The path to his destiny

In *The Alchemist*, Santiago's quest to find the treasure actually leads him to find himself. Each character he encounters and all of his experiences help to further his quest to fulfil his destiny, meaning the "mission" that each individual was put on earth to accomplish, which will allow them to find inner harmony. According to the king of Salem, everyone knows what their destiny is as a child, but little by little "a mysterious force begins to convince them that it will be impossible for them to realize their destiny" (p. 20).

Sure enough, throughout the story Santiago is faced with a variety of obstacles and temptations, all of which test his will and serve as learning experiences. It only by overcoming them that he manages to find his treasure, thus fulfilling his destiny. These obstacles include:

- His money being stolen, meaning that he is forced to work for the crystal merchant in order to be able to continue his journey.
- The tribal war that leaves the caravan stranded at the oasis. The young shepherd is left with no

way of staving off boredom except watching the desert and the birds of prey that live there. In fact, a hawk triggers his vision of an army invading the oasis, which means that he is able to warn the inhabitants of the imminent danger.

- When he meets Fatima, "the Soul of the World surge[s] within him" (p. 88).
- When he is arrested by the soldiers, Santiago performs a miracle and turns himself into the wind. The soldiers are so impressed they offer the alchemist and his pupil an escort so that they can travel safely to the Coptic monastery.

Another characteristic that allows the story to be categorised as a coming-of-age novel is the fact that Santiago has a number of encounters with other characters who help to further his quest and allow him to gain a deeper understanding of himself. These characters include:

- the king of Salem, who advises him to make his own decisions;
- the camel driver who advises him to live in the present;
- the alchemist, who acts as his guide and companion.

Although the young shepherd is unaware of it, each of these encounters and all of his experiences bring him closer to fulfilling his destiny.

THE FANTASTIC

Stories which involve supernatural elements are generally categorised as "fantasy" or "fantastic" stories. These elements take the form of unusual phenomena which do not seem to obey the natural laws of our world and cannot be explained through science. They interact with reality by means of occult sciences such as alchemy or magic, premonitions or certain forms of religion.

One of the genre's defining characteristics is that it tends to borrow a wide range of elements from different cultures: "Fantasy encompasses the magical and the miraculous, which gives it significant anthropological density. This is because fantastic motifs are nourished by our religious, epic, ancient, Celtic and esoteric imaginations [...] creating an aesthetic which borrows from a wide variety of traditions"[1] (Aron, Saint-Jacques and Viala, 2010: 387). Characters are guided by

---

1. This quotation has been translated by BrightSummaries.com.

higher powers, and the events depicted in the novel require the suspension of the reader's disbelief, meaning that even though they know that what is being described is impossible, they accept it as real within the context of the story.

In this novel, the protagonist's character development is constantly guided by elements of fantasy. His first encounter is with the king of Salem, who knows Santiago's entire life story even though they have never met before. He tells the shepherd how to get to Africa and gives him Urim and Thummim, "the only form of divination permitted by God" (p. 66). In fact, many fantasy stories feature similar episodes at the start of the story in which a mysterious but powerful figure gives the hero a magical object which will help them to fulfil their destiny.

Later on, at the end of the book when Santiago has almost reached the Pyramids – meaning that he is on the verge of fulfilling his destiny – he is able to speak to the desert, the wind ("The wind approached the boy and touched his face. It knew of the boy's talk with the desert, because the winds know everything", p. 139), the sun and the universe itself in turn, and all of them respond to him, which enables the young man to turn himself into wind and show that he can enter the Soul of the World. Here, Coelho is using a prosopopoeia, which is a stylistic device often used in fantastic stories in which inanimate or abstract objects are made to speak.

CRITICAL RECEPTION

A hybrid novel

It is difficult to determine the literary genre that *The Alchemist* belongs to. Some critics have classed it as a philosophical tale, while others prefer to categorise it as an esoteric work or even a book about personal development. Coelho has described himself as "a storyteller, and believes that his books should be placed on the literature or philosophy shelves of a bookshop"[2] (Arias, 1999: 155). Meanwhile, Nicolas Brucker, who performed a sociological study which analysed how the book was received among students in Lorraine (France), describes the novel as a "book of wisdom"[3] (Brucker, 2003).

---

2. This quotation has been translated by BrightSummaries.com.
3. This quotation has been translated by BrightSummaries.com.

Criticism and public recognition

Coelho is relatively unconcerned about the lack of critical recognition his books have received in terms of their literary merit: "I believe that the success of my books, many of which have ambiguous meanings, is partially due to the way that they let the reader see themselves reflected in these characters undertaking spiritual journeys. My books are full of these signs"[4] (Arias, 1999: 38).

In fact, many readers have contacted Coelho to tell him how much his work has moved them. Some of them see the author as a guru, but Coelho makes a point of distancing himself from such labels because he views spirituality as a personal matter. Similarly, in *The Alchemist*, Santiago meets characters who guide him during his quest by offering him suggestions, or even by shedding light on certain matters which he was previously unaware of, but the young shepherd makes his own decisions and answers to no one.

4. This quotation has been translated by BrightSummaries.com.

THEMES

Travel

Santiago goes on a veritable pilgrimage in order to fulfil his destiny. At the very start of the story, travelling is described as "his purpose in life" (p. 7), and in order to fulfil it, he defies his father by becoming a shepherd instead of a monk. This allows him to spend two years roaming the lands of Andalusia until "he knew all the cities of the region" (p. 8).

However, he soon feels a budding desire to travel further afield, and he imagines that one day he could sell his sheep and become a sailor. In the end, he has a dream which guides him on a journey through Tarifa, Tangier, the desert and an oasis, all the way to the Pyramids of Egypt.

This journey allows Santiago to discover other cultures and foreign landscapes: "The desert was all sand in some stretches, and rocky in others" (p. 71). When he returns to the place he started from to dig up the treasure, Santiago wonders why he could not have been spared all the trouble, but a voice replies that without it, he would never have seen the Pyramids: "'No,' he heard a voice on the wind say. 'If I had told you, you wouldn't have seen the Pyramids. They're beautiful, aren't they?'" (p. 160). Furthermore, he would never have met Fatima. In other words, Santiago understands that the treasure's value also lies in the obstacles he had to overcome in order to find it.

Religion

Santiago is Spanish and a Christian. He studied theology and was supposed to become a priest, but he discovers another religion, namely Islam, during his time in Africa.

When he arrives in Tangier, Santiago sees "women with their faces covered, and priests that climbed to the tops of towers and chanted – as everyone about him went to their knees and placed their foreheads on the ground" (p. 32), and inwardly describes these Muslim customs as "practice[s] of infidels" (*ibid*.).

Santiago learns more about Islam while talking to the crystal merchant, who explains that the Muslim holy book is called the Koran and teaches him the Five Pillars of Islam (pp. 51-52):

- there is no God but Allah, and Mohammad (c. 570-632) was his prophet;
- every Muslim must pray five times a day;
- every Muslim must fast during Ramadan (a month when believers must abstain from eating, drinking, smoking, wearing perfume and having sex between sunrise and sunset);
- every Muslim must give charity to the poor;
- every Muslim who is financially and physically able to do so must go on a pilgrimage to Mecca at least once in their lifetime.

Alongside the references to Islam, there are also allusions to Christianity, as a church features in the plot and there is a reference to Saint Santiago Matamoros (p. 32). The Englishman also talks about a story from the Bible (the adoration of the shepherds in the Gospel of Luke), and other biblical references are scattered throughout the novel: Melchizedek (the name of one of the kings of Jerusalem who is mentioned in the Old Testament), King of Salem, Urim and Thummim (stones which are carried by the High Priest of Israel in the Hebrew Bible), and so on.

The Englishman does not seem to be a believer: when the leader of the caravan asks everyone to swear obedience to the God they believe in, the Englishman remains silent. However, he is able to quote the Bible, meaning that religion is mainly mentioned as a cultural touchstone.

Love and women

When Santiago meets Fatima, the main female character, it is love at first sight:

> "At that moment, it seemed to him that time stood still, and the Soul of the World surged within him. When he looked into her dark eyes, and saw that her lips were poised between a laugh and silence, he learned the most important part of the language that all the world spoke – the language that everyone on earth was capable of understanding in their heart. It was love. Something older than humanity, more ancient than the desert. Something that exerted the same force whenever two pairs of eyes met, as had theirs here at the well." (pp. 88-89)

Santiago is so overwhelmed by this encounter that he forgets about his destiny – he could easily have stayed at the oasis, dismissing the Pyramids and the treasure buried under the sand there as a mad dream. However, the alchemist says that "love never keeps a man from pursuing his destiny. If he abandons that pursuit, it's because it wasn't true love... the love that speaks the Language of the World" (p. 115). Fatima, who symbolises the concept of love, does not act as an obstacle for the young shepherd, who decides to return to the oasis after he finds the treasure.

The author felt that it was essential to include women in the novel, because he believes that women represent "the sacred, she is the energy [...] the logic of mysteries, of the incomprehensible, of the miraculous"[5] (Arias, 1999: 110). In Eastern philosophy, the masculine and the feminine are believed to play a crucial role in maintaining the balance of the universe, and the old fortune-teller that Santiago visits at the start of the novel reappears at the end, because he owes her a debt which could cause an imbalance and prevent the young shepherd from fulfilling his destiny if it goes unpaid. However, when he gives the old woman a tenth of his treasure, he will be able to leave and be reunited with Fatima.

---

5. This quotation has been translated by BrightSummaries.com.

LITERARY CONTEXT

A simple style

Coelho's style is characterised by its utter simplicity, both in terms of narrative structure and in terms of syntax and vocabulary.

Firstly, the narrative follows a linear structure, with the events unfolding in chronological order. There are only two exceptions to this rule, namely the two short flashbacks at the beginning of the novel, which depict his encounter with the daughter of a textile merchant and the day he told his father he was leaving the seminary to go travelling.

Secondly, the novel uses accessible vocabulary and keeps complex, specialised terms to a minimum. Even when Coelho is describing aspects of Islam which might not be familiar to all his readers, he uses Westernised vocabulary by calling the muezzin a "priest" (p. 32) and the minarets "towers" (*ibid*.).

New characters are always introduced separately: every time a new main character is introduced, the previous one disappears, except during the section when Santiago is accompanied by the alchemist, as they encounter a group of soldiers and then the monk together. The author comments on this technique in Santiago's internal monologue: "If he ever wrote a book, he thought, he would present one person at a time, so that the reader wouldn't have to worry about memorizing a lot of names" (p. 15).

Intertextuality

The Alchemist contains a wide variety of cultural, theological and literary references. According to Gérard Genette (French essayist, born in 1930), this writing style is a form of transtextuality, which can be defined as "all that sets the text in a relationship, whether obvious or concealed, with other texts" (Genette, 1997: 1).

There are many references and allusions within the novel which act as clues informing the reader about Coelho's own experiences as a reader. For example, in the preface to certain editions of the novel, the author states that he "paid homage to the great writers who were fluent in the Language of the World: Hemingway [American writer, 1899-1961], Blake [English poet and artist, 1757-1827], Borges (who also based one of his tales on Persian history) and Malba Tahan [pseudonym used by the Brazilian writer Júlio César de Mello e Souza, 1895-1974], to name but a few"[6] (2007 French edition: 17-18).

Furthermore, when a reedition of the novel was published, Coelho wrote a new foreword to the novel in which he reminisces about how difficult it was for him to start writing *The Alchemist*. He says that one day, he was looking out the window and saw an old sailor aboard his boat, which reminded him of *The Old Man and the Sea* (1952) by Ernest Hemingway, a novel in which the protagonist is called Santiago. This thought proved to be the inspiration he needed to start writing: "And I knew, in that magical moment, that there was a book hidden in those simple words"[7] (*ibid.*: 9).

Coelho mentions yet another writer in his preface: Oscar Wilde. In fact, the first time the alchemist appears in the novel, he reads

---

6. This quotation has been translated by BrightSummaries.com.
7. This quotation has been translated by BrightSummaries.com.

a short story by Wilde which is based on the myth of Narcissus, which also provided inspiration for Ovid's (Roman poet, 43 BCE-17/18 CE) *Metamorphoses* (1/2 CE).

Literature within the novel

Coelho places a great deal of importance on books as objects, on the act of reading, and on writing as a symbol of fate:

- *The Alchemist* goes beyond the concept of literature and also explores the concept of the book as an object. As a shepherd, Santiago can only carry around the objects which are absolutely vital for his survival – even his coat seems unbearably heavy to him during the hottest hours of the day, and he has to remind himself that he will need it that night. Santiago reads one book at a time, using it as a pillow at night and exchanging it for a new one when he has finished reading it. When the king of Salem approaches him, he uses the new book that Santiago is reading as a pretext for starting a conversation, because although reading is a solitary activity, it also provides readers with a means of connecting with each other. Santiago never actually finishes this book, which begins with someone being buried under snow: he leaves it in the desert, because it is "an unnecessary burden" (p. 72). This shows that a person's destiny can only be fulfilled by following the signs, not by clinging to material objects.

- Melchizedek is able to write the young shepherd's life story in the sand, even "things that he had never told anyone" (p. 20). This convinces Santiago that the old man really is the king of Salem. The alchemist knows "the secret of the Master Work" (p. 63), which "could be written simply on an emerald" (p. 120), and can write in the sands of the desert. In fact, it is the desert that allows Santiago to enter the Soul of the World.

- Once Santiago has arrived in Africa, a number of the people he meets use the Arabic word "Maktub" (pp. 56, 74 and 93), which can be translated as "it is written" or "it is fated". This means that Santiago must decipher the signs in order to read, and therefore fulfil, his destiny. By using an untranslated word from a foreign language to convey this idea, the idea itself takes on the air of a magical formula, which only initiates like the alchemist can understand.

- The shepherd must learn to speak the "Language of the World" (p. 144) so that he can pray to "the hand that wrote all" (*ibid.*) as the sun counselled him to do in order to save his own life. He is then able to communicate with the Soul of the World, which is the Soul of God.

This vision of writing as a means of communicating with the universe echoes Coelho's own writing process. He explains that he feels ready to write following a kind of mental gestation "after making love to life"[8] (Arias, 1999: 158). According to Coelho, writing is a means of sharing, and this is how he communicates with his readers.

The Alchemist is a bestselling novel which has sold over 65 million copies. It has been translated into more than 50 languages in around 150 countries, and a film adaptation of the novel has been planned. However, it is not simply a literary phenomenon: many readers have been personally affected by Santiago's story and have

---

8. This quotation has been translated by BrightSummaries.com.

taken the novel as an invitation to embark on a quest to fulfil their own destiny.

FURTHER REFLECTION

SOME QUESTIONS TO THINK ABOUT....

- In your opinion, why is this novel named after the alchemist even though it tells Santiago's story?
- In this novel, what are the similarities and the differences between the ways different people view dreams? More broadly speaking, in what ways do dreams play a key role in an individual's life?
- What role do women play in the novel?
- How much importance is placed on nature in the novel? What role does it play, and what message does this convey to the reader?
- How are elements of fantasy incorporated into the novel? What do they add to the story?
- What does the concept of destiny mean? Is fulfilling your destiny a question of fate or of free will? Justify your answer.
- Travelling is one of the main themes of this novel. Why does Santiago wish to travel at the

beginning of the novel? Has he discovered everything he wanted to by the time he returns?

- Throughout the novel, Santiago must make choices. Who or what does he rely on when he is making these choices? In your opinion, how free are we to make our own choices?

- In what respects is *The Alchemist* a coming-of-age novel?

- The fortune-teller tells Santiago that "[i]t's the simple things in life that are the most extraordinary" (p. 14). What does she mean by this? Do you agree with this message?

We want to hear from you!
Leave a comment on your online library
and share your favourite books on social media!

FURTHER READING

REFERENCE EDITION

- Coelho, P. (2012) *The Alchemist*. Trans. Clarke, A. R. London: HarperCollins.
- Coelho, P. (2007) *L'Alchimiste*. Trans. Orecchioni, J. Paris: J'ai lu.

REFERENCE STUDIES

- Arias, J. (1999) *Conversations avec Paulo Coelho*. Paris: Éditions Anne Carrière.
- Aron, P., Saint-Jacques, D. and Viala, A. (2010) *Le dictionnaire du littéraire*. Paris: Presses universitaires de France.
- Brucker, N. (2003) Usage et culture du livre de sagesse : L'Alchimiste de Paulo Coelho. Enquête sur les pratiques de lecture des étudiants de l'Université de Metz. *Hal.archives-ouvertes.fr*. [Online]. [Accessed 22 February 2018]. Available from: <https://hal.archives-ouvertes.fr/hal-01242325>
- Encyclopaedia Britannica. (No date) *Types of novel: Apprenticeship*. [Online]. [Accessed 22 February 2018]. Available from: <https://www.britannica.com/art/novel/Types-of-novel#ref51004>

- Genette, G. (1997) *Palimpsests: Literature in the Second Degree*. Trans. Doubinsky, C. and Newman, C. Nebraska: University of Nebraska Press.

MORE FROM BRIGHTSUMMARIES.COM

- Reading guide – *Veronika Decides to Die* by Paulo Coelho.

www.brightsummaries.com

Ebook EAN: 9782806273284

Paperback EAN: 9782806273291

Legal Deposit: D/2015/12603/588

Cover: © Primento

This guide was written with the collaboration of Johanna Biehler and translated with the collaboration of Emma Hanna for the character study of the alchemist and for the sections "Alchemy", "A young hero searching for himself", "The fantastic", "Critical reception", "Love and women", "Intertextuality" and "Literature within the novel".

Digital conception by Primento, the digital partner of publishers.

Printed in Great Britain
by Amazon